LEVEL 1

Jack's Game

Rod Smith

 **Richmond** READERS

⬔ **Richmond** READERS

LEVEL 1

(500 headwords)

Maria's Dilemma

Oscar

Jack's Game

The Boy from Yesterday

The Black Mountain

LEVEL 2

(800 headwords)

Jason Causes Chaos

Craigen Castle Mystery

The Road through the Hills and othes stories

Where's Mauriac?

Saturday Storm

LEVEL 3

(1200 headwords)

A Trip to the Stars

Dr Jekyll and Mr Hyde

The Canterville Ghost and Other Stories

Cold Feet

Frankenstein

LEVEL 4

(1800 headwords)

A Trip to London

Dracula

Jane Eyre

The Adventures of Tom Sawyer

Sense and Sensibility

LEVEL 5

(2600+ headwords)

Steve Jobs: the man behind Apple

Elizabeth II The Diamond Queen

Jack's Game

Laura deLuce is happy in her new job at the Butramex agrochemical* company in Kelowak, western Canada. Then, one day, something happens. No one explains what. Her boss* says she must stay away from the office. The Indians on the reservation are angry with the company. What is going on? Laura starts to investigate...

....

Rod Smith is a writer and teacher. He is from Oxford, England, but now he lives in Paraguay with his wife and young son. When Rod is not writing, he likes playing the piano or taking long walks in the country.

LEVEL 1

10th April

Today was the first day of my new job. It didn't begin very well. The weather was bad. It rained all day, without stopping. But something interesting happened.

I got to work twenty minutes early. The rain was heavy and I didn't want to get wet. So I waited in the car. Five minutes later, a man came out of the offices where I'm going to work. He was tall, with red hair, and he wore* a long white coat. He walked out into the rain and went to look at the flowers in front of the building.

I watched him. I was interested.

'Why is he standing in the rain?' I thought*. 'And who is he talking to? The flowers?'

I waited a short time and then I got out of the car. I went up to the building. The man with red hair looked at me. When I saw* how big he was, I felt* a little afraid.

'Hello,' he said. 'Are you the new girl - Laura deLuce?'

'That's right,' I answered. I felt better. He had a nice face.

'Hello,' he said. 'Are you the new girl - Laura deLuce?'

He didn't tell me *his* name. He said, 'Maybe you think I'm not normal, but don't be afraid of me.'

'Of course not. But I, er...'

'You want to know why I'm standing in the rain, talking to the flowers, don't you?' He was right, but I didn't say anything. 'It's because of my little garden,' he said. 'The rain means spring is here. It also means that it's not so cold. And this part of Canada is usually very cold.' He looked down at the flowers. 'The white ones are *Puschkinia scilloides, "Alba".*'

'And the others?' I asked.

'*Scilla sibirica* – a beautiful blue flower. Early this morning, when I saw the rain, I came out to see them. The warmer weather is a big change for them. So I talk to them. They like that. Here–' He went to take one of the flowers.

'Er, no, thanks,' I said. I didn't want to walk into my new job with a flower in my hand.

He looked down at his plants. 'The new girl doesn't like me,' he said.

'Oh no, you mustn't think that,' I said quickly.

'That's OK.' The man laughed. 'But don't stand here in the rain. We can talk later.'

I said goodbye and walked into the building. 'Is everyone that works here like him?' I thought.

There was a woman at reception. When she saw the expression on my face, she laughed. 'That's Jack,' she said. 'He's always playing games.'

■ ■ ▪

16th October

That was six months ago. I often think of that day – my first day in the company.

I was happy then. I'm not now. The situation is different – like Jack. It's interesting, isn't it? When I first saw him, I thought he was very strange*. Now I think he's my only friend.

------ CHAPTER 1 ------
The Message

17th October

Something is wrong, something here, in the office.

It's early and I'm the only person in the room. I look at the clock on the wall. It's dark and the numbers are difficult to see. I don't want the lights on, so I move nearer. Nearly seven o'clock in the morning. I'm here early because I have a lot of work to do. But I can't work. I feel that something is not right. I need to know what it is.

Is it the two people I work with? Jack, whose second name is Kincaid, and Fallon, Mike Fallon. Jack works in the laboratory next door. Fallon works here, in the office. Yesterday, I thought they were both ill. They walked around the building like very old people and their faces were very white.

'Are you OK?' I asked Jack.

'I'm fine, thanks,' he said, and laughed.

Fallon said nothing.

I like Jack. He's an interesting man. He knows the Indians that live on the reservation near here. They have a lot of apple trees. When the trees are not looking well, which sometimes happens, he likes to help them. Jack knows a lot about plants. The Indians like him because he studies their problems. But I think there is something more than that. I don't know what it is. Maybe they like him because he's a big, happy man who laughs a lot.

Not like Fallon. Fallon is a computer programmer from Chicago. He's a cold, angry man. I don't like him. And he doesn't like me. I think it's because I'm a young woman with an important job. I'm also tall and he's short. Fallon doesn't like that.

Sometimes I watch him sitting at his computer. I see his fat hands and small dark eyes moving over the keyboard. All day he writes programs, types in information and analyses it. 'Poor man,' I think. 'Work is the only thing in your life.' He's a company man, you see. Fallon does anything the company asks.

I'm different. I like my job, but I don't like the company.

It's called 'Butramex'. It's an American company. They[•] make agricultural fertilisers. They also do

---

[•] *When we refer to a company as an institution, we use the pronoun* it; *when we refer to the people who work for the company, we use the pronoun* they.

All day he types in information. His small dark eyes move over the keyboard.

experiments. That is why they are here. They say they are doing this work because they want to help people in poor countries. I don't think that's true. I think they only want to make money.

Some people in the town don't like what the company is doing. They say it's bad for the environment*. A few months ago some of these people formed an environmental group. This group does not accept the information the company gives about its experiments. They want to know what happens in this building. But they can't get in. No one can. Not without identification. There's a high fence around the building and security guards at the main gate. I'm not happy about the situation.

Is that what's wrong? Is it because I'm not happy here? Because I'm not happy with Fallon? Or is it the company and the work I do?

No, it's not only these things. Today there is something more. Something about this office which is different. What is it?

Cold, grey light comes through the windows. I look at the things around me once more. Were they like this yesterday? Or–

I stop. Something white, like a human hand, moves at the back of the room. At first, I'm afraid. But then I see what it is – a piece of paper.

A piece of paper comes out of the printer. Who is it for?

It is coming out of the printer. I am surprised. Why is the printer working? I'm the only person in the building. Or am I? Slowly, I walk across the room. I take the piece of paper and read it.

```
File* name: JG
Username*: XXX
Print: 22.00
Message: XOT = OIIH
```

I don't understand. Who is this for? And what does it mean?

I hear someone speaking. It's Mike Fallon. He's saying hello to someone outside the office. I put the paper in my desk. I can look at it later when there is no one here.

Fallon comes into the office.

'Hello,' I say.

He moves his head, but he doesn't answer. There is an angry expression on his face. He turns away from me and sits at his computer. He begins to work. What a strange man.

CHAPTER 2

At the Reservation

It's half past eight. I'm standing by the window. The telephone rings*. Fallon is not in the office so I answer it.

'deLuce?' It's my boss*, Oscar Strode.

'Yes?'

'I want to see you in my office.'

Strode is a good example of a bad boss. He never says please. There is no one in the company I like less. But I mustn't think like this. It doesn't help.

'When do you want to see me?' I ask.

'Now.'

'OK.' I put the phone down. What's wrong?

Jack's laboratory is next to my office. Maybe *he* knows what is happening. I go into the laboratory. It is empty. I go to the window and look down at Jack's little garden. There's no one there. 'That's strange,' I think, 'Jack is usually here in the morning.'

Five minutes later, I'm opening the door of Strode's office. I see there is another person there - Fallon. He is standing on the other side of the room, looking out of the window.

'Sit down,' says Strode. He is a tall man with cold, blue eyes. They look at me without moving. What is he thinking? It's impossible to know. His face is hard and empty, like a wall.

I sit down. 'Is anything wrong?' I ask.

Strode speaks without answering the question. 'You must help Fallon this morning. He's going to the fields near the reservation. But I don't need you this afternoon. Or tomorrow. Some people are coming to study the work we do here. It's important that the building is empty while they do this. You can stay at home. Wait for me to phone before you come back to work. And don't worry* – you're not going to lose any money.'

He looks at Fallon. Fallon walks quickly across the room. He has the keys to one of the company cars. He gives them to me.

'You can drive,' he says.

■ ■ ■

The fields are fifteen kilometres from the company's office. Butramex uses them for its fertiliser experiments. I am a fast driver, so we get there quickly. I stop the car. Fallon gets out.

'Wait here,' he says. 'I can call when I need you.' He walks away, carrying a box full of small bottles. I don't want to stay in the car, so I get out and watch him go across the first field. I don't watch for long. The area around us is more interesting.

To the right of the fields is the reservation fence. To the left is a river. In spring, when ice* breaks, the water carries pieces of ice down from the mountains. At that time the river is like a busy road, with strange white cars moving along it. The Indians call it *Chumaluk,* the

White River.

I watch Fallon putting soil* from the ground into different bottles. He walks slowly with his head down. I look away. I am sorry that I don't like the man.

Something moves, to my right. I see a group of Indians, standing outside the reservation fence. They have angry expressions on their faces. One of the Indians comes forward and shouts at Fallon. Fallon looks up. The next second a stone hits him on the arm.

Fallon walks quickly back to the car. 'Let's go,' he says.

I stand there. I am so surprised that for a moment I can't move.

'Come on!' Fallon shouts. I can see that he is afraid.

In the car I ask about what happened. But Fallon doesn't want to tell me. Maybe he doesn't know.

We drive to the company without speaking. I stop outside the office and give Fallon the keys. He leaves without saying goodbye.

I get my car from the car park and drive home.

■ ■ ■

I live in a small apartment in the centre of Kelowak. Kelowak is a town in the west of Canada, not far from the company. Most people that work for Butramex live in Kelowak. My apartment is at the top of a tall building. From my window I can see the White River and the mountains behind it. After a day at work, I like to look at these things. When I do this I feel calm.

A group of Indians standing outside the reservation fence have angry expressions on their faces.

Usually.

But today I can't relax. I know something is wrong at work and I want to know what it is. I sit down and try to find answers to the things that happened today.

First, I remember feeling that there was something wrong in my office. Then there was the strange message* that came out of the printer. (Why did I leave it in my desk? That was not very intelligent of me). A short time later, I went with Fallon to the Butramex fields. Then I came home.

'Wait for me to phone before you come back to work,' Strode said. What a strange thing for Strode to say - he usually wants people to work hard. Finally*, out at the fields, one of the angry Indians hit Fallon on the arm with a stone. Why? What does it all mean?

I look at my watch. It's 1.45p.m. Jack goes home for lunch at one o'clock. I can call him. Maybe he knows what is happening. I go to the phone. And then I remember another thing. I didn't see Jack at work this morning. Is he ill? He looked ill yesterday.

The phone rings for a long time. Jack doesn't answer. Where is he? I put the phone down. I feel worried.

What can I do? I think that all the strange things that are happening are part of some big problem. But how can I learn what it is?

I don't need to think for long. I know that there is only one way to find out. I must get into the company. But not now. It is better to wait. Fallon goes home at

around eight o'clock. He is always the last to leave. I
can go then.

■ ■ ■

I stand at the window and look at the mountains. I feel
calmer now. Maybe this is because I know what I'm
going to do.

⑤ ——— Chapter 3 ———
The Night Visit

At seven-thirty that evening I leave my apartment. The
roads are busy and it takes longer than usual to drive to
the company. I park my car at the bottom of the road
which goes to the main gate. I begin to walk. There
are trees all round the security fence. I stay behind the
trees so that no one can see me. When I get to the
underground car park doors, I stop. This is the plan: I
stay behind the trees; Fallon drives out; I run through
the automatic doors before they close; I get into the
Butramex building through the car park.

I sit on the ground and wait.

I don't wait for long. At half past eight the doors
open and a car drives out. I move back in surprise. It is
not Fallon's car, it is Strode's. Strode is driving. Fallon
is sitting beside him. He looks worried.

At half past eight the doors open and a car drives out.

The car goes past. I run from the trees and into the car park. The doors close behind me and everything goes dark. I find the wall and move slowly along. Soon the wall ends. This is where the stairs are. I don't want any night guards to hear me. So I take off my boots and walk quickly up to the third floor.

It is not so dark when I get to my office. This is because of the electric light which comes through the window from the area of the main gate. I look out of the window. I see a night guard. He is sitting on a chair with a newspaper over his face. That means he is sleeping. Good.

I take off my boots and walk quickly up the stairs to the third floor.

I go to my desk. When I sit down, again I get the feeling that something is wrong. Something small, but important. What is different about this office? I look around the room again. But I can find no answers in the things I see.

And then I remember the message in my desk. Is the answer there? I take it out and begin to study it, more carefully this time.

```
File name: JG
Username: XXX
Print: 22.00
Message: XOT = OIIH
```

I look at the characters again, but I cannot understand them. Then I look at the top of the print-out. Maybe the file has other information which explains them. I see that the file is called JG. But next to 'user'[*] – the person who sent[*] the message or the sender[*] – there is no name. Why is that? And there is another strange thing. The time on the print-out says 22.00. But it printed at 7.00a.m. Why?

I turn on[*] my computer. I type some letters and numbers on the keyboard. A list of all my files comes onto the screen. None of them has the name JG. I'm not surprised – the message wasn't sent to me. Maybe it was for Fallon? I go to his computer and turn it on. I find nothing. Fallon's computer has no file with the name JG. This means that the message wasn't sent to

Fallon. So who *was* it sent to?

I go to my computer. I want to find answers to my questions, but I don't know how. I sit down. 'Come on, Laura,' I say, 'you're not being a very good detective.'

I type the characters XOT = OIIH. I look at them, big and white on the dark blue screen. I stay like that for a long time. But they mean nothing to me. Finally, my eyes get tired and I look away.

An idea comes to me. I can try to get into Strode's office. Maybe the information I need is in there. I go to the window and look down. There is no change: the guard is sleeping like a child.

I go back to my computer. I stop when I see something on Fallon's computer screen. Did I forget to turn it off*? Maybe. But then I see what it is I'm looking at. It's the characters on my screen, reflected on his. I see them in reverse: HIIO = TOX. The first letter is an 'H'; the second looks like a '2' in roman numerals; the third is an 'O'. Of course! Now I understand. The sender used a very basic code*. He or she put everything in reverse. When the characters are reflected on Fallon's screen, I see them correctly. Now, for the first time, I know what they mean. 'H2O' is the chemical symbol for water. The equals sign (=) means that the water contains* something. And that 'something' is toxic. 'TOX' is part of the word 'TOXIC'. Now I see what is wrong in my office. I look around again. The plants are dry and the room is

It's the characters on my screen, reflected on Fallon's screen.

very quiet. There is not the usual sound of water moving through pipes*. That is not surprising. The water is turned off. And now I know why, too. The water is turned off because it contains something toxic. That was why Jack and Fallon looked so strange yesterday. They had some toxic water and they were ill.

A thousand questions come into my head. How did this happen? Who found out about the toxic water? Was it the sender of the message? Why did they write in code? Why did they put 'TOX' and not the full word 'TOXIC'? Who was the message for? Why was it sent at ten o'clock at night? And why did it print at seven o'clock in the morning? Why didn't it print at the correct time?

I look at the characters once more. Something dark moves across the screen.

It is the shadow* of a man.

———— C H A P T E R **4** ————
Where is Jack?

I turn. A man is standing by the door. Is it a security guard? I don't know. It is dark and I can't see very well. But the man sees me. He comes into the room. I think he is going to hit me. But I am not afraid – I am a big girl.

I move quickly to the left. Then I take the man's arm and turn it behind his back, hard.

'Stop – please. Friend,' he cries.

I see it is not a man, but a boy. He is about seventeen years old. I take my hand away from his arm. 'Who are you? And what are you doing here?' I ask.

The boy waits for a moment. Then he speaks. 'My name is Jim,' he says, 'Jim Sawchuk. I am from the reservation. I work here in the evenings. I clean the offices.'

'So why are you moving around in the dark?'

'Because no one must see me.'

'Why not?' I am angry.

'Wait. I can explain,' says Jim. 'Yesterday evening,

I take the man's arm and turn it behind his back, hard.

when I came to work, something strange happened. Your boss, Mr Strode, was at the main gate. All the office buildings behind him were very dark. He explained why. "All the lights are off," he said. "There's a problem with the electricity. You can go home. Don't come back before you hear from me.'"

A problem with the electricity? Strode didn't say anything about that to me. And I know why. It wasn't true. He said it to stop Jim coming to work.

'This morning, Strode sent me home, too,' I say. 'I'm here to find out why.'

'Now I know who you are,' Jim says. 'You're Laura – Jack's friend. He talked about you.'

'Jack? Where is he? Do you know?'

'No. The last time I saw him was the day before yesterday. But none of us knows where he is now.'

'Us? Who's "us"?'

'The people in the environmental group. Jack is in the group, too. He gives us information about what the company is doing. But, of course, no one in the company knows about this. Except you…'

'Don't worry,' I say. 'I'm not going to tell anyone. But you must tell me what you're doing here.'

Jim looks at the printer. 'I came to look for a message. From Jack.'

'This message?' I move to the computer.

Jim looks at the characters, then he looks at me. 'Maybe,' he says. 'I don't understand Jack's messages. They are always in code. For security. One of the others in the group reads them. The only thing I understand is the JG.'

'And what does that mean?'

'Jack's Game - it's the name of a file. We keep the information that he sends us in it. It was Jack's idea. He loves playing games.'

'I know.' I remember my first day at work.

Jim looks at me. There is a question in his eyes.

'You want to know how I got the message. Right?'

'That's right,' says Jim.

'The message came out of the printer at seven o'clock this morning. Now I think I know why.' More answers come into my head. 'Last night, Jack began to type the message into his computer. Someone - maybe Strode or Fallon - went into the laboratory and saw him. Jack quickly sent the message. He typed 22.00 next to "print", the time when you are usually here. But Strode turned off the electricity to stop you working. The electricity came on again early this morning. And at seven o'clock this morning the message came out of the printer. It was nine hours late - because of the problem with the electricity.'

We are quiet for a moment. Jim looks very serious.

'Is anything wrong?' I ask.

'Yes,' Jim says. 'Where is Jack now?'

'I don't-' I hear a noise* and stop speaking. The noise is coming from outside. We go to the window.

The guard is not sleeping any more. He is standing in front of his office. A big, black car is driving through

A big, black car is driving through the main gate.

the main gate. It is Strode's car. Strode is driving. Fallon is sitting next to him.

There is a gun in Fallon's hand.

―――― CHAPTER **5** ―――― ⑦

In the Tunnel

'Come on,' I say to Jim. 'They know we're here. Let's get out of this place.'

We leave the office and run down the stairs. We must get out through the car park before Strode and the others find us.

But we are too late. When we get to the ground floor, Fallon is inside the building. He sees us. We continue down to the car park. I know that my plan can't work now. There is no time to open the automatic doors before Strode and the others catch us.

Jim looks at me. He knows what I'm thinking. 'Don't worry,' he says. 'I know a route. Let's go.'

'Where are we going?' I ask.

Jim doesn't answer. We get to the car park and close the door at the bottom of the stairs. Jim takes something from a box on the wall. The lights go out.

'Now there's no electricity,' he says. 'That gives us a little more time.'

'But without electricity we can't open the automatic doors.'

'Don't worry,' Jim takes my hand. 'Come with me.'

We run across the car park. Jim, like most Indians, sees well in the dark. Where is he taking me? How did he get *into* the building? Did he get in the same route as me? No, that's not possible. Strode's car was the last to leave.

I hear a door open. Then I feel stairs under my feet. We start to go down. The air is dark and cold.

'Is this the way you came in?' I ask.

'No. I came in through the car park.'

'How? I came in after the last car went.'

'I was here before you. I waited downstairs. When the guard was asleep, I came up to the offices.'

'So where are we going now?'

'To where Butramex get their water.' Jim explains. 'There is a tunnel under this building. When the river is high, it isn't easy to get into the tunnel. Part of the White River runs through it. The water is cold, because of the ice, and it runs very fast.'

'So what are we going to do?' I ask.

'We must wait at the bottom of the stairs. When the others leave the building to look for us-'

'Listen.' I stop on the stairs. Jim stops, too. 'Can you hear that?' I ask.

We hear the sound of voices. They come from far away. 'Yes. I can hear Strode and the others,' says Jim.

'And that's all. Right?' I ask.

'Yes. What do you mean "that's all"?'

'It's strange. The river runs through the tunnel.

"Very fast," you said. So why can't we hear it?'

'You're right,' says Jim. 'That is strange.'

We get to the bottom of the stairs. Yellow light comes through a door in front of us.

'The electricity is on again,' says Jim.

I say nothing, and listen. All is quiet. We wait for a moment. Then we walk towards the light.

We go through the door and into the tunnel. The walls of the tunnel are black and wet but there is no water running through it.

'Where's the river?' I ask.

'I don't know. I don't understand this,' says Jim.

'Here. Over here.' We hear a man's voice, to the right.

We begin to walk up the tunnel. The tunnel lights are not very good. We move slowly, getting nearer to the voice. After a few metres I see a man near the right wall of the tunnel. It is Jack. His hands and legs are tied with rope.

We untie* the rope. Jack stands up with our help. He looks tired and ill.

'I'm happy to see you two,' he says. 'But how did you know I was here?'

'We didn't,' I say. 'We came down here to escape from Strode. He and Fallon are looking for us. And Fallon has a gun.'

'I know,' says Jack. 'Last night he hit me with it.'

'What happened?' Jim asks.

Jack looks at us. I can see that he is angry. 'I was

31

His hands and legs are tied with rope.

busy in the laboratory yesterday,' he says. 'I was analysing the water. It was almost eight o'clock when I identified the problem. Eight o'clock is late for me - I usually leave work at six. Strode and Fallon thought that maybe someone from the environmental group was in the laboratory. So they came into the room to see who it was. Fallon had a gun. I sent the message before they got to me. Strode asked me, "Why are you here so late?" I didn't answer. Then he looked at Fallon. Fallon hit me on the back of the head with the gun. They carried me down here and tied my hands and legs with rope.'

'What about the river? Jim said the river–'

'Listen to the whole story,' says Jack. 'About two weeks ago, the Indians saw that there was something wrong with their apple trees. They were very angry. They knew it was because of the Butramex fertilisers in the fields next to the reservation. At that time Strode wasn't worried - the Indians couldn't prove* anything. But it was different when the fertilisers got into the river. After a few hours the water was toxic. The Butramex buildings use the river water, and many of the people that work in the company got ill. And then Strode was worried. I can imagine what he thought. "What happens when the newspapers find out about the toxic water? What happens to my job?" So he turned off the water.'

'How?' I ask.

'Look at this,' says Jack. He takes a piece of paper

The Indians saw there was something wrong with their apple trees.

from his jeans and gives it to me. It's a plan of the tunnel. 'Do you see these two things?' Jack asks. 'At the right end of the tunnel?'

'Yes,' I say. 'What are they?'

'They are hydroelectric generators. The force* of the water coming through the tunnel works the generators. They give electricity in an emergency. Below them are two big metal gates. The gates control the force of the water.'

'And what is this long thing, next to the gates?' I ask.

'That's a ladder. The ladder goes up from the bottom of the tunnel, through a door in the roof. Below the

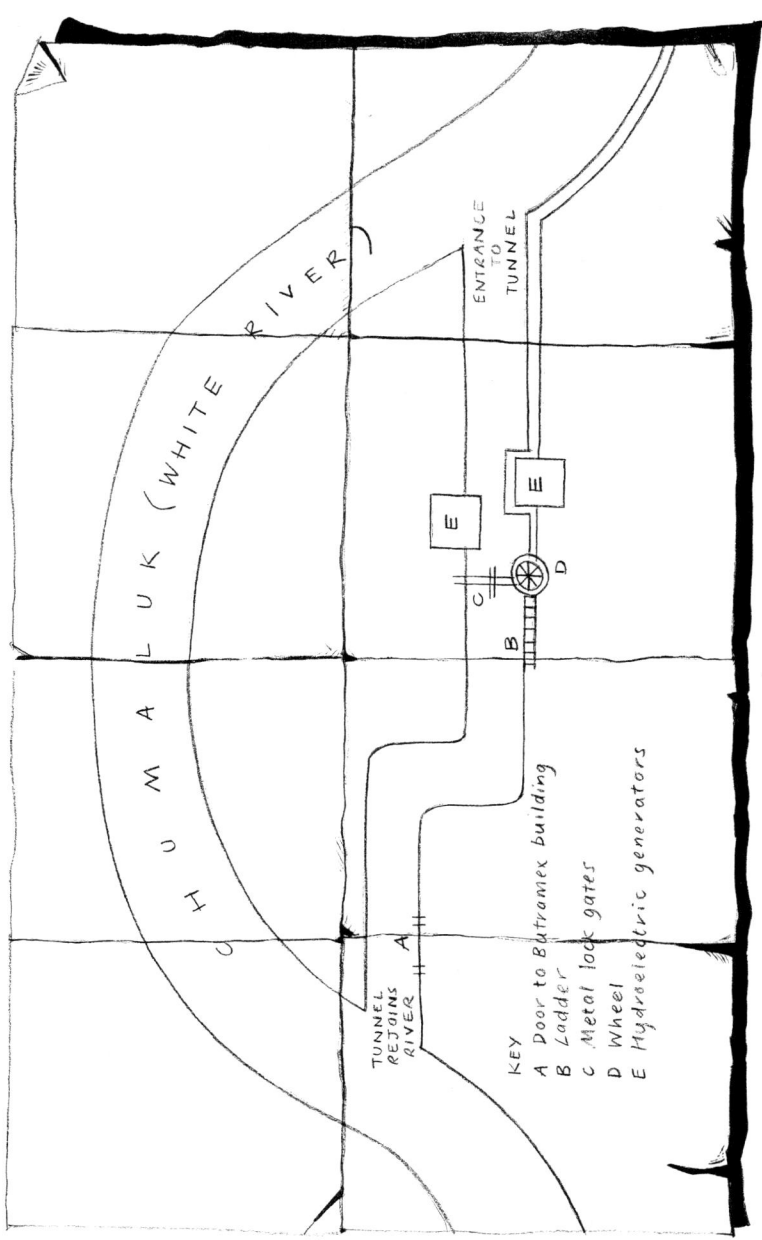

CHUMALUK (WHITE RIVER)

ENTRANCE TO TUNNEL

E

E

C

D

B

A

TUNNEL REJOINS RIVER

KEY

A Door to Batromex building
B Ladder
C Metal lock gates
D Wheel
E Hydroelectric generators

roof there is a wheel which opens and closes the gates. Yesterday, Strode came down the ladder, turned the wheel and closed the gates. He wanted to stop the water coming in. When all the toxic water passes down to the sea, he can open the gates again.'

I want to ask more questions, but I hear voices. They are getting closer. 'It's Strode,' I say. 'He knows we're here. Is there a way out of the tunnel?'

Jim speaks suddenly. 'Yes,' he says. 'We can go up the ladder at the end of the tunnel and get over the gates. There is a path, next to the river, on the other side of the gates. We can follow the path and get away.'

We hear voices behind us. Strode and the others are in the tunnel now.

'Good,' says Jack. 'They are going away from us, to the left. Let's move.'

We start to run. Jack can't run very fast. Jim puts a hand on his arm and helps him. The tunnel turns to the right. We hear Strode and the others coming back.

'We can't do it,' says Jack. 'It's because of me. I can't run very fast. But I can stay here and–'

'NO!' Jim and I cry at the same time.

We stop running. Jim takes his hand from Jack's arm. 'We can all stay,' he says, quietly.

'There they are.' It's Fallon's voice. 'Don't move!'

Jim turns and looks at Fallon. 'With the gun you feel important, don't you, Fallon?' he says. 'But you are not important. You are a small, sad man who has no friends.' Jim moves towards Fallon.

Fallon moves back. He is afraid. 'Stay there!' he cries. 'Jim. Wait,' says Jack.

But Jim doesn't listen. 'The company is your life, Fallon. But it is not your friend.'

Suddenly, there is a shot*. Jim falls to the ground.

'Oh no,' says Jack. He sits down and puts his hand on Jim's head. 'Come on, old friend,' he says. But Jim doesn't move.

The gun falls from Fallon's hand. His face is very white. He stands next to the guard, watching.

Suddenly, there is a shot. Jim falls to the ground.

Jack stands up. He is very angry. He walks towards Fallon and kicks* the gun away. Fallon is more afraid now. The guard tries to help him but Jack knocks them both down. Their heads hit the tunnel wall and the two men stay on the ground. They don't move.

For a moment, everything is quiet.

But then there is another shot. And this time Jack falls.

Someone moves from the shadows of the tunnel. It's Strode. The gun is in his hand.

What can I do? Jack and Jim are dead. I can't help them now.

The guard tries to help Fallon but Jack knocks them both down.

I begin to run again. I know I must try to get out of the tunnel before Strode kills me.

A few metres away the tunnel turns to the left. I run on and see the gates in front of me. The ladder is on the right. The wheel is next to it, below the roof. I have an idea. I get to the ladder and I begin to go up. I hear Strode coming after me. I look down and I see the gun in his hand. I get to the top of the ladder. I don't think about the gun.

I turn the wheel. It is heavy, and difficult to turn. A shot goes past my head. But I don't stop. I turn, turn, turn.

Seconds later, there is a loud noise. The noise is like

The noise is like a mountain, falling into the sea.

a mountain, falling into the sea. I look down. The gates are open now. All I can see is water. Far away, I hear a cry. Then there is nothing. Only the noise of the angry White River.

Cold air hits my face. I turn my head and look over the gates. I see the night sky through a big round hole about thirty metres in front of me – the end of the tunnel. I climb over the gates and run towards the open air.

(8) ————— EPILOGUE —————

10th April
Six months later
Butramex is closed now. The police closed it the day after Jack and the others died.

I left my job and went home. Now, one year after it all started, I am here again. I don't know why. Maybe because it's 10th April, the day I met my old friend.

I stand in front of the office building. It is different now. There are no fences to stop people getting inside. The Canadian government uses the building now. They use it for environmental work. Nothing is secret. The people of the town can visit the area and there are no guards with guns. Everything is different.

Well, almost everything. One thing is not different - Jack's little garden. I look at it now, full of blue and white flowers. They move slowly in the wind and I see something for the first time. It's a name – *Scilla* – spelled in white in a sea of beautiful dark blue. Someone planted the flowers like that. And I know who.

Dear Jack. Always playing games.

Someone planted the flowers like that. And I know who.

EXERCISES

A Comprehension

Chapter 1 The Message

1 Why is Laura at the office early?
2 Why does Laura think that Jack is 'interesting'?
3 What do some people who live in the town think of Butramex?
4 What does Laura see at the back of the office?
5 Why is she surprised?

Chapter 2 At the Reservation

Put these five sentences in the right order.

1 An Indian hits Fallon on the arm with a stone.
2 Laura decides to go back to the company.
3 Strode tells Laura to come to his office.
4 Laura phones Jack. He doesn't answer.
5 Fallon gives Laura the keys to one of the company cars.

Chapter 3 The Night Visit

1 Fallon drives out of the car park. True or false?
2 The lights are on in Laura's office. True or false?
3 The guard is reading a newspaper. True or false?
4 People in the company are ill from the water. True or false?
5 Laura doesn't know what 'JG' means. True or false?

Chapter 4 Where is Jack?

Complete these sentences.

1 When Laura sees that Jim is a boy, she...
2 Strode sent Jim home because...
3 Jim last saw Jack...
4 Jack sends his messages in code...
5 After they hear a noise, Laura and Jim...

Chapter 5 In the Tunnel

l Why is there no water in the tunnel?
2 What happened to Jack after he sent the message?
3 Why were the Indians angry?
4 What is at the right end of the tunnel?
5 Strode tries to kill Laura. How does Laura kill Strode?

B Working with Language

l **Use these words to join the pairs of sentences below:**
   so   but   and then   because
a Laura was early for work. She waited in the car.
b Strode rang Laura. He wanted to see her.
c Laura went to Jack's laboratory. He wasn't there.
d Jim and Laura went into the tunnel. They saw Jack.
e Jack was angry. He hit Fallon.
f Laura climbed over the gates. She got out of the tunnel.

2 **Put these sentences in the correct order.**
a Fallon killed Jim.
b Strode wanted Laura to come to his office.
c Laura saw a message come out of the printer.
d Laura opened the gates in the tunnel.
e An Indian hit Fallon with a stone.
f Laura got into the Butramex building through the
   underground car park.

3 **Find as many words as you can related to computers in**
   Jack's Game. **Draw a simple outline of a computer. Label**
   your picture with words you find and other words you
   already know.

C Activities

1 When Laura got out of the tunnel, she telephoned the police. Write down their conversation.

2 Imagine you work for the environmental group. Write to the Canadian government and explain why you think Butramex must close.

3 Imagine Laura didn't kill Strode, but Strode killed Laura. How does he explain the five bodies - Fallon, the security guard, Jack, Jim and Laura - in the Chumaluk River to the police?

GLOSSARY

agrochemical *(adj)* the company make chemical products, such as fertilisers, for agriculture

boss *(n)* informal word for the person you work for

code *(n)* a secret form of communicating

contain *(v)* to have something inside; e.g. 'This glass *contains* water' means 'This glass has water inside it.'

environment *(n)* the natural world; **environmental** *(adj)*

felt *(v)* past tense of *feel*

file *(n)* *(computing)* a compartment on disc in which to keep documents or other information

finally *(adv)* we use *finally* to introduce the last thing in a series of things happening

force *(n)* how strong something is

ice *(n)* solid water

kick *(v)* to use your foot to move something violently or hurt someone/thing

message *(n)* a piece of information communicated by one person to another

noise *(n)* something we hear

pipe *(n)* tubular metal through which liquid can travel

prove *(v)* to demonstrate with evidence

ring *(v)* the telephone *rings* when someone is calling you

saw *(v)* past tense of *see*

send *(v)* to cause something to go from one place to another

sent *(v)* past tense of *send*

sender *(n)* person who sends* a message*

shadow *(n)* a dark place where light cannot fall; a person makes a *shadow* on the ground when he or she walks in the sun

shot *(n)* a gun fires a *shot*

soil *(n)* the top layer of the ground; plants live in *soil*

strange *(adj)* unusual; difficult to explain

thought *(v)* past tense of *think*

turn off *(v)* to stop something working, e.g. the electricity

turn on *(v)* to start something working, e.g. a computer

untie *(v)* opposite of *tie*, meaning to put something around someone so they can't move

user *(n)* *(computing)* the person who is operating the computer

username *(n)* identification when signing onto a computer

wore *(v)* past tense of *wear*

worry *(v)* to feel concerned about something